I Collect Rocks

By Sunita Apte

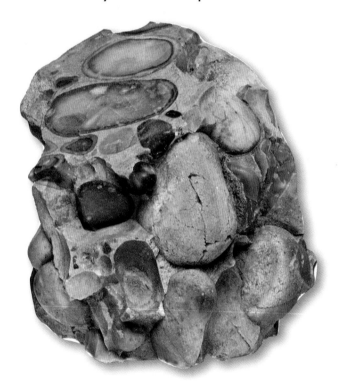

Scott Foresman
is an imprint of

Glenview, Illinois • Boston, Massachusetts • Chandler, Arizona •
Upper Saddle River, New Jersey

Photographs

Every effort has been made to secure permission and provide appropriate credit for photographic material. The publisher deeply regrets any omission and pledges to correct errors called to its attention in subsequent editions.

Unless otherwise acknowledged, all photographs are the property of Pearson Education, Inc.

Photo locators denoted as follows: Top (T), Center (C), Bottom (B), Left (L), Right (R), Background (Bkgd)

Opener: ©Macduff Everton/Corbis; **1** ©Andreas Einsiedel/©DK Images; **3** ©Blair Seitz / Photo Researchers, Inc.; **4** (Inset) ©Julie Woodhouses/Alamy Images, (Bkgd) ©Patrick Robert/Sygma/Corbis; **5** ©Patrick Robert/Sygma/Corbis; **6** ©Harry Taylor/©DK Images; **7** ©Macduff Everton/Corbis; **8** ©Andreas Einsiedel/©DK Images.

ISBN 13: 978-0-328-46391-6
ISBN 10:   0-328-46391-4

10 11 12 13 V010 18 17 16 15 14

I like to collect rocks.
I collect all kinds of rocks.

I collect big rocks.

I collect small rocks.

I collect shiny rocks.

I collect bumpy rocks and smooth rocks.

All my rocks are interesting.

I collect rocks that were once sand.

I collect rocks made
of fossils.

I even collect rocks made of other rocks.

I found this one by a river.

What do you like to collect?